To Mue

GW01452532

Take Me To
Point Nemo

Stephen Selby

Thanks for coming
and for being an
inspiration.

Steve XX

1

Photograph on page 9 courtesy of Sheila Selby

Other books by the author

Sunrise

To Ladye Bay and Back

Instagram

@steveselbysteveselby

"We are the Riders on the Storm".

"For a time, I believed that mankind had been swept out of existence and that I stood there alone, the last man left alive".

H.G. Wells

Contents

Nanjizal- Towan- Porth Nanven- Remembering Rebecca-
The Sound Of Water

Into The Light- Will I Still Be Here?- The Café- In The
House Of God- Today Is A Sunny Day- The New View- All
Was Good

Pastures New- Autumn Blossom- At Last- As Beautiful-
Nirvana- As Yet Unwritten- Riders On The Storm- Beyond
The Altar- The Mist Has Now Cleared

The Poetry Bench.

Introduction

In his dreams, meadows of wildflowers led towards high cliff tops. Violent waves crashed against the cliffs below. He often stood here, looking out to sea. Dreaming of Point Nemo.

He thought of nothing but Point Nemo. He imagined a life away from civilisation, a thousand miles from any human existence. Here he would be freed from all of life's struggles and worries. He believed this would be his nirvana.

Was this how he would end his days? Alone in paradise? Maybe, this would be a new beginning. Point Nemo, the place where his dreams could finally come true. Where he could escape from the cruelty of the world and the state it was in.

Located in the South Pacific, Point Nemo lies more than two hundred kilometres from the nearest land. What a place it must be, but how hard it must be to find. One day he believed he would make it there. He would finally escape from all of life's hardship and conflict. There would be no more judgement, no more anxiety, no more pain. Point Nemo was where he wanted to be.

The isolation sounded ideal. The sight of the stars at night would be spectacular. This was the perfect place to see out his days. To be free from the world. To reach a place of peace and tranquillity. However, he harboured doubts.

Maybe isolation wasn't the answer. With no food, no land and no possibility of escape, it seemed clear that any settlement would be short-lived. The possibility of seclusion from the world may have sounded idyllic but loneliness would soon hit home.

Maybe, life was not as bad as he had thought. Maybe. he was missing so much beauty in the world. Maybe. people weren't as cruel and heartless as he had believed. Maybe. he just needed to give life a chance.

First, though. he had to experience whatever life wished to throw at him. To endure the hard times. To wait for the turning of the tide. Only by doing this would he fully appreciate the beauty of the world.

Finally, he would emerge into the light, and he would see that the world was as beautiful as any happy ending. With his thoughts now redeemed of all uncertainty and confusion, he would see that the mist, at last, had cleared.

Saved from the horrors of Point Nemo, he would be free to venture onwards, in search of pastures new.

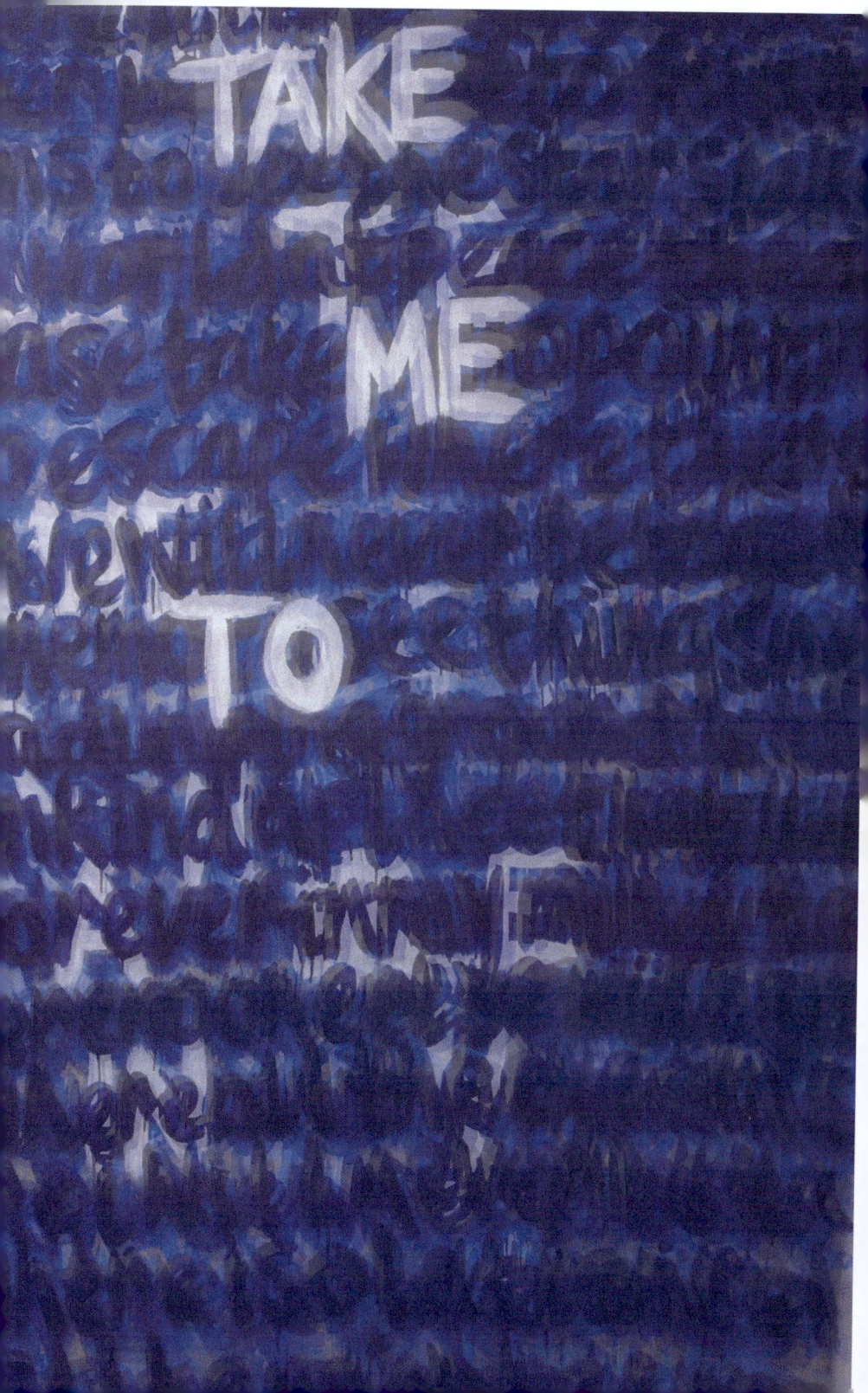

TAKE
ME
TO

Part One

Take Me To Point Nemo

We're all islands shouting lies to each other across seas of misunderstanding.

Rudyard Kipling.

Take Me To Point Nemo

Take me to Point Nemo
Where no one else will go
Away from all insanity
Where all the eye can see is sea
A place where I will never be

Take me to Point Nemo
Where isolation reigns
To see the stars like ne'er before
The sky lit up, a world at peace
The one place I could find release

Take me to Point Nemo
From where there's no escape
Where there can be no resolution
Where love could never last forever
Where we will never be together

Take me to Point Nemo
To see things never seen
A world unfound, a dumping ground
A thousand miles from humankind
A place that I will never find

A place forever in my mind.

Wildflowers

I long to wander where wildflowers grow
Where land meets sea, where cliffs rise high
To indulge in my passion, whilst the chance still
remains
To immerse in the scene as I lay down to die
My path has led me to this bittersweet choice
As the sun starts to fade, and the darkness sets in
I will toast to the glory of the world one last time
Look above, back to where life is yet to begin
Reminisce in the peace of this view of my past
To remember when life wasn't filled with such pain
Then accept my release, know it's time to let go
To be freed from this trauma, not to face it again
The darkness descends, I can no longer see
There will not be a sunrise, at least, not for me.

To Be So Tall

To be so tall, to be a freak
To stand out in the crowd
Oh, to be small, not so unique
To not stand tall and proud

My head may well be in the sky
But I still hear your cruel jibes
The questions which you throw at me
Bring vicious, nasty vibes

You think you're funny with original wit
But I'm sorry to break your delusion
I've heard your jokes a thousand times
Your humour is just your illusion

To be stared at by day, to be talked of by night
The paranoia you cause isn't fun
Anxiety. panic, whenever I'm out
I feel trapped by your comments but I'm too nice to
run

No, I don't want to talk about Peter Crouch
And no, I don't play basketball
I'm fifty years old and out of shape
I'm sure the NBA won't give me a call
And no, my mum didn't make me sleep in a grow bag
And yes, my bed is way too small
And, yes, it's hard to get clothes which fit
And no, my parents are not that tall
And no, it isn't cold up here
And, yes, I struggle to sit on a plane
And, please, stop playing guess my height

Your inane questions drive me insane

Call me Daddy Longlegs or BFG
Or the Green Giant, is it fun mocking me?
I'm too polite to say enough is enough
So, I nod along but my laughter's a bluff
But, you know, I've had it with your insults and cheek
And your cringeworthy comments, you sound so naff
And. yes, I duck to get through doors
And you know it already, but I'm not a giraffe

And sometimes, yes, I bang my head
But the headaches are nothing next to listening to you
If you think I'll let my height define me
I'm afraid you don't know me; you don't have a clue
I'm worth more than a number, I'm sure others agree
I won't answer your questions, you're far too mean
But as you've asked so many times
The shoes on my feet are a size fourteen

So next time you see me and fancy a natter
I'm not a freak show for your jokes and your mirth
Learn some manners or keep your mouth shut
And stop acting like my height is all I am worth.

Because I'm A Man

Because I'm a man- I tried to act tough
I hid from my feelings, but enough is enough
I cat-called, wolf-whistled, as women passed by
Tits out for the lads was my favourite cry
With my drinking buddies, I'd down gallons of beer
No time to reflect, my aim was quite clear
Another notch on the bedpost to prove I'm a man
To find love and contentment was never my plan
So, I'd cheer on Clarkson, he's a splendid bloke
And if people got hurt, well, it was only a joke
The only valid existence, one where I was pissed
The only language I knew, came straight from the fist
To me, women were objects, to be treated as such
My life was a play, but the act was too much
Oh, the act was so shallow but why should I care?
When I'm having such fun? Far too drunk, unaware
Of my feelings inside, so, I hid from the world
Then I hid from the pain and my problems unfurled
When I ran from my demons they dug deeper inside
So, I hid from it all, but found nowhere to hide
I had tried to impress, be what I couldn't be
To be something ridiculous, to be anyone but me
So, I'm left in this cesspit, alone and distressed
But I'll never accept that I'm feeling depressed
The pretence and the acting are all that I know
But, behind the scenes, the tears start to flow
All the pressure to conform, has left me a wreck
Will it leave me destroyed, with a noose round my
neck?
But there's still time to change, time to talk, to admit
To my inner most feelings, before I choose to quit
To take responsibility, time to carry the can
To face up to my problems, because I am a man

No Way Out

There is no way out
No magical cure
No way of escape
Through a secret door
No chance to transport me
To a safe place today
The wind will not lift me
Or blow me away
The tide takes me out
But it turns far too fast
Then it brings me right back
To a bittersweet past
Whilst the world is turning
I am left behind
As others move on
I'm confused and confined
To a place where no one
Can hear me shout
I am lost in the mist
There is no way out.

Unending

I dreamt last night; I was running free
Full of vigour and vibrant with hope
Bounding with energy, a sense of self worth
Instead, I'm bedridden, unable to cope
Too tired to sleep, too tired to live
Fatigued and empty, my life on hold
Laid up in bed, chained to the past
My dismal present, my outlook cold
My bones they ache, can't climb the stairs
Fall to the ground, on knees I crawl
Withdrawn, afraid, my fate imposed
The pain too much, I've hit the wall
Was this my path? To end this way?
With countless nightmares and broken dreams
The worry, doubt, at what's to come
Where no one listens to my screams
As morning comes, I'm drained of hope
Despite the sun, I'm tired as night
The pain unending, I'm on my own
Descending deeper, I've lost this fight
When will this end? So soon, I hope
The spasms, headaches, each day the same
The pain, the guilt, the lonely cries
Lie deep inside me, I hide in shame.

Anyone But Me

Would I find myself a happier place
If instead of this, I'd been born a girl?
Would my head be in a better space
If I'd tried to climb a different hill?
Released from all these empty feelings
Which penetrate me deep inside
Instead of feeling such a failure
I'd face the world with strength and pride
The empty nights are long and lonely
The loneliness is cruel and real
My inner thoughts, destroy the silence
No chance to think, no time to heal
A constant sense of disillusion
Forever tired and full of dread
Can I escape the isolation?
Where endless nightmares fill my head
The aches and pains might disappear
Fatigue and apathy fade away
Concentration might be regained
A different view, on a different day
I wish I had the capability
To feel your love and in return
To satisfy and make you happy
And not be ruled by false concern
Don't make me face the dying sun
Don't watch me suffer all alone
Don't make me battle what I face
Don't let me do this on my own
Then I will face the fading light
My faith restored but still not free
My final conclusion, one hard to accept
The way to be happy, to be anyone but me.

The Fork

A fork in the path and I can't decide
In the deep, thick haze there is nowhere to hide
One way, my redemption, I've been led to believe
The other, damnation, no chance of reprieve
Is there really a choice to be made in this place?
A path to freedom and a chance to shine
A place I've dreamt of for far too long
With the haze never-ending, is the choice really
mine?
The mist, it seems, will never lift
As darker clouds begin to descend
The path I choose, it changes nothing
Whichever I take, I am facing my end.

Part Two

The State We Are In

"We live in a world where we have to hide to make love, while violence is practiced in broad daylight".

John Lennon.

The State We Are In

No one to vote for- Not much to hope for- Surrounded by hate- No way to escape- So much has regressed- So many depressed- The tension and stress- But still, I digress

The sky falling in as panic sets in- A world full of sin- The state we are in- The bad guys- The dream dies- Are we even alive? - What's the ultimate prize?

We face extinction- Plagued by addiction-A world full of friction- Of contradiction- Computer games- And social media- Farewell to the Encyclopaedia

The twitter wars- To settle scores- What total bores- Your life not yours- The Facebook-The Tik Tok- Where to look? -The ticking clock- Time running out- Controlled by louts-Too late to shout- Of that, no doubt

Hatred, bigotry on the rise- Come on guys- Be wise- No surprise- Society dies- Plot their demise- And screw their lies

Teenage suffering- Mental health smothering-Failures uncovering- It's terrifying-The knife crime- Lives on the line- Lost in their prime- Before their time

The food banks- The poor give thanks- We're firing blanks- A nation of cranks- Protests negated- The working class hated- The poor castrated- Society weighted- To favour the rich- Roll over you bitch

The people on strike- Denied their right- To a decent days pay- There's nothing to like- Our leaders deny us-

They really despise us- But those in power- To whom we cower- Those bastards empowered- Throw them in the tower

The rich get richer- Do you get the picture? -The poor on their knees- Are left to freeze- By energy bills-Which give the chills- It's one big con- All hope is gone- Their profits skyrocket- We've got empty pockets- They've fooled us all- In this cold war- We do as they say- Defeated today- We've given in- Believed their spin- Thrown in the bin- They're under our skin- Took it all on the chin- We let them win

The state we are in.

All Your Fault

It's the fault of striking nurses; they will do just as
they please
With their greed and self-importance, bring the
nation to her knees
It's the fault of the downtrodden, they will never pay
their way
They scrounge, enjoy their benefits, then spend their
days at play
It's the fault of single mothers, for not keeping their
legs closed
For their shameless, slutty lifestyles, with their selfish
lies exposed
It's the fault of the disabled, with the duty which they
shirk
We've heard all the excuses, for God's sake do some
work
It's the fault of the homeless who bring squalor to the
street
Spread disease and awkward feelings to everyone
they meet
It's the fault of the migrants, invading on their boats
These terrorists, insurgents, have us all held by our
throats
It's the fault of the teachers who no longer want to
teach
And the lazy home workers spending summer on the
beach
It's the fault of the food banks and the fraud that they
inspire
Let them starve to death, these peasants, in their
squalid, putrid mire
It's the fault of bloody cyclists and their ill-conceived
green wars

The heart bleeding environmentalists, run them down
in your four by fours
It's the fault of every one of you, for daring to exist
If all of you disappeared today, then none of you
would be missed
And to you, the striking nurses, get down on your
knees and serve
And show respect, to people like me, there is nothing
you deserve.

Retail Park

A scene of desolation
Where nothingness pervades
Surroundings full of misery
Of soulless, mawkish trades
The centre of oblivion
Where only cars can go
A lonely vacuum, a sterile place
How did we get so low?

The miserable dual carriageway
The roundabout to Hell
Is this the way we're heading?
To humanity's death knell?
Characterless- designed to depress
A depravity of the soul
A void of shallow emptiness
Where nobody feels whole

Charm free cinemas, tasteless food
We've been fed this web of lies
Sports Indirect, the staff abused
We all ignore their cries
Bank Holiday joy? It's all a ploy
A lifeless place- designed to destroy
But still we go, we let this transpire
Abandoned our souls on this funeral pyre

Lost in the car park, we're truly doomed
In this world so aloof and full of doubt
Drowned in this senseless, morbid state
Where humanity will be wiped out.
The game is up, it's too late now
We chose this path, the future black

We made our bed, we'll die in it
The Retail Park, no turning back.

I Heard They Killed Some White People In Gaza

I heard they killed some white people in Gaza
You couldn't have failed to notice
It was plastered over the press
I read that they were aid workers
Guiltless victims with hearts of gold
The bombs left desolation, an unholy, blood-filled mess

I heard they killed some white people in Gaza
The bombs they dropped from up above
They bought from us- or so I'm told
The western world was furious
We said we may withdraw support
For the misuse of our weapons- the ones which we had
sold

I heard they flattened hospitals in Gaza
They said it was a Hamas base
We said, "feel free to carry on"
The buildings blown to kingdom come
The sick were slaughtered in their beds
The bombs they kept on falling until everything was
gone

I heard they killed some babies in Gaza
The survivors left as orphans
The bombs continued raining down
Well, carry on and win your war
But next time, could you help us out
Please make sure that the victims of your bombs and
guns are brown.

President Nero

He fiddled as Rome burnt to the ground
Some say it was he who lit the match
18th July AD 64
One thousand nine hundred and sixty years passed
In all those years, not much has changed
Despite all that's happened, the world still the same
The narrative remains unaltered
Still led by tyrants by a different name

The lower classes loved him
But he never had their backs
Always looking for someone to accuse
Through lies and smears and attacks
He castigated Christians
Now others take the blame
The constant search for scapegoats
It hides a deeper shame
His tyranny compulsive
Corrupt and self-obsessed
The world bowed down in reverence
Held under his arrest

Some celebrated when he died but others claimed it
wasn't true
They say that evil never dies
We'll never start this world anew

He fiddled as Washington burnt to the ground
As violent riots hit the streets
They all believed the words he said
All the blame he apportioned, all the lies he fed
As the final embers of the fires that burnt
Were lost in the wind on that fateful day

In his speech the rabble cheered him on
Immersed in delusion, his evil held sway

All he predicted, all the lies he sold
It all came true, or so we've been told
Dethroned, still strong- they still believed
We thought he was gone, we felt relieved
But in defeat he sought revenge
A nation divided, a nation at war
No room for debate, no chance of escape
We've seen how this all unravels before

The crazy stories, the crazy theories
Insipid leadership brought us here
With no solution on the table
The only hope, to wish him dead
But as shots were fired, he turned his head
He was still alive, the fiddler survived
He rose from the ground to cheers from the crowd
He raised a fist, he looked so proud
And the worry now is what lies ahead

Hand him the keys to a world under siege
Let him break more laws
Let him start new wars
What could have been his last hurrah
Has seen him rise into the stars
A living martyr, what awaits
In a world where his lunacy dictates
Send him to prison, condemn him to Hell
He'll never be beaten, we're under his spell

We thought his reign was over but, no, it wasn't true
They say that evil never dies

We'll never start this world anew
We thought that he was gone for good but now he will return
And again, the fiddler will fiddle as he watches Rome burn.

Arboretum

Different shades and different colours
Rising high towards the light
Some stand bare, some full of vigour
Through the winter, through the night

Come the spring, we smell the blossom
Come the summer, trees of green
Come the autumn, swathes of colour
Every day, a changing scene

Universe of trees and flora
Blossomed through the years of time
Made by man, but with the knowledge
Knowing he'd not see her prime

Ours to relish, ours to savour
Not to plan or to assess
Ours to leave the planet poorer
Desolate and in a mess

In the future what awaits them?
All we've tarnished won't mature
To the young, we leave you nothing
A dying world which won't endure

Arboretum, watch you burning
Left as embers on the ground
Live today, forget the future
The stench of failure, all around.

One Hundred Years

One hundred years from now
Who knows what might remain?
Where floods abound on lower ground
Where fires rage, destroy, rampage
The things we hold so close
The things we love the most
Are dying fast, we'll soon be toast
A downward trend, we'll never mend
We've gone too far, we always are
And always were, forever will
Be pushing the boundaries again and again

But deniers they cry, we'll never die
You're all so wrong, we'll always live on
They'll never notice when profit's their motive
When now is now is now is now is now
Is all that seems to matter somehow
The world now burning as fast as it's turning
The world is sinking, too fast for our thinking
We watch it die and still do nothing
We keep on going but know we're struggling
With nowhere to go, who really knows
In a century from now, then where will we be?

It terrifies me.

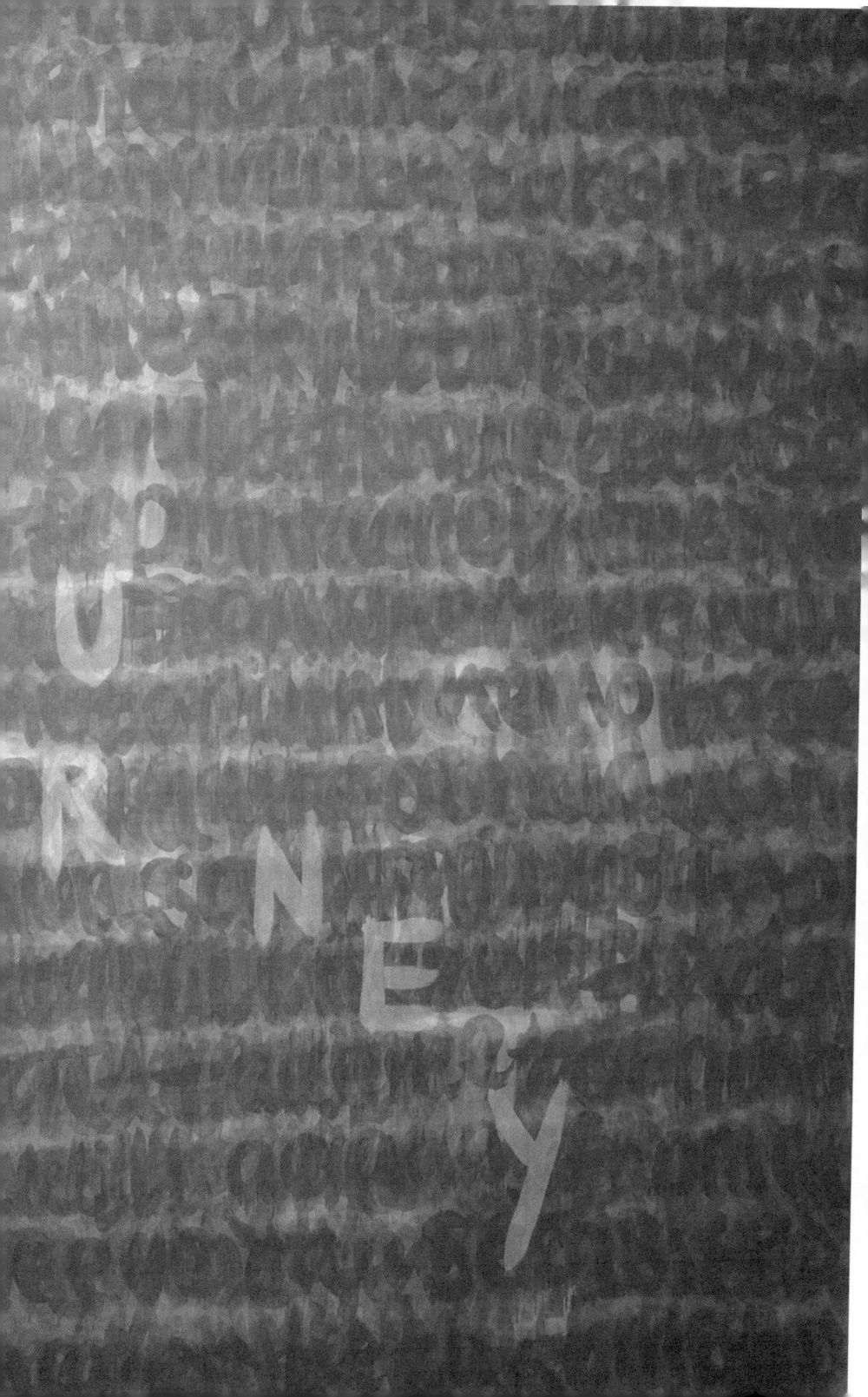

Part Three

The Journey

"The journey, not the destination matters."

T.S. Eliot.

The Journey

The windows mist up, obscuring my view
Of the world all around, as I leave without you
Through villages, past farmland, there's a long, long
road ahead
Everything seems distant as I face the trip with dread
Is this all a fantasy? Are these places even there?
I see it all from far away, it's not a world I wish to
share
So soon the things I saw are gone with a different
view revealed
But the new view, too, is fleeting, with all thoughts
and hopes concealed
Everything is changing, I start to think, "what's really
here?"
As my memories mist over, nothing in my mind is
clear
Perhaps I imagined it all before? Perhaps the sun
disguised my past?
Perhaps the hazy backdrop formed a fantasy which
couldn't last?
The windows to my past confused, whichever way I
look
The view before me. all a lie, from a journey which I
never took.

And Then I Found My God

And then I found my God

And the oceans parted as I recognised the truth
And the world around me, finally, seemed to make
sense
And everything now had a purpose
And everything I saw was good
And everything meant everything
The joys of life seeped through my veins
New revelations cleansed my soul
The day I found my God

Then all the colours of the rainbow
Merged into one in front of my eyes
And what I saw was incredible
And what I saw was indelible
And all I saw was beautiful
The day I found my God

And was it a coincidence
On that cloudless, sunny day
That euphoria swept over me
As the fates began to swallow me

And there sat by my side
At last, I found my God
Exactly as I imagined he could be
In the place where I had been taught he would be
He was all that I expected
When my soul, had been infected
He was all that I rejected
When my heart had been neglected

Then I opened my eyes wide
Despite everything I had denied
He had waited there for me
He created this world for me

Through years of rumours and Chinese whispers
Where all that's good had been ignored
But all the things that I'd been taught
And all the paths that I'd been shown
About this God I'd never known
All turned out to be true

All the plaudits I had earned
All the lessons I had learned
All the places I had been
All the faces I had seen
As I looked up to a heavenly sky
They all disappeared in the blink of an eye
And beyond the stars, looking down on me
Was a God I had never wanted to see

Then, when I found my God
I walked on water, turned water to wine
I rose from the dead, he forgave my sin
At last, a new life was about to begin
An eternity of nothingness
A void of shallow emptiness
An abyss where all are envious
He stretched as far as the eye could see
This world not created in his image
His image created in this world
As a realisation dawned on me
I took a moment to reset
The loss too hard to justify

I wanted badly to forget
I felt no resignation
Just a feeling of what's meant to be
The feeling not a depression
But an acceptance of my destiny

Bow down to fictions of imagined worlds
Marvel at imagery of angels in clouds
Where all I see is what I want to see
Where all I'll be is what I long to be
Where we can sense no empathy
When we're consumed by jealousy
Then we will adhere to a higher command
When we are blind to all that's true
When we can lie, yet still have faith
Then we can be happy
Escape our mortality
Condemn all those in the world below
Savour sensations they will never know
Plan for a future that is all for show
Accept an existence where we'll never grow

In my slumber I was woken by the demons from my
past
As the darkness of yesterday came to haunt me at
last
And all that I believed came from clouds up above
I ascended into Heaven with my heart drained of all
love
And I felt a sense of sorrow as I entered Heaven's
gates
I was forced into repentance and surrendered to the
fates

Then I looked down on a world, I would never get to
see
As I begged for mercy from my God in the hope he
might love me.

Glastonbury

I watch them board the buses
Clean and fresh and raring to go
Full of life, anticipating
Where smiles and laughter fill the air
Ready for their trip to Hell

What drives them to this wretched place?
Where the chance to sleep is just a dream
To be awake to face their nightmares
The queues, the crowds, the mud, the noise
A place which they cannot escape
They signed up to this dreadful fate

Returning exhausted
They smell like a sewer
The tents abandoned; litter strewn
I understand none of this
But even so, I find myself
Wishing I could be there
Wanting to be part of what they have
To enjoy what they enjoy
To find pleasure where I find nothing
To share their camaraderie, their spirit
To not feel so alone

In the words of Kurt Cobain
"I wish I was like you
Easily amused"
For me no laughs, I cannot smile
I cannot comprehend
The world I'll never share
How can I judge?
When I love nothing

When I feel nothing
When I have nothing
When they have everything
The world in their hands
Then me, a mere spectator
Watching from afar
Detached and out of touch
I can never imagine
The magic in their world
The joy they all feel
A life of simple pleasures

I envy them all.

My Punishment

This will be my punishment for everything that I have done
No choice but to concede that there is no escape, no place to run
Technically, I wander free, but captive still, against my will
Chastised, despised and ill-advised, where all is over-analysed
Tarnished by humiliation a victim of retaliation
A cell with no walls, no boundaries at all
I'm down on the floor with no one to call
Cold and defenceless, no self-esteem
Undignified, flawed, were my actions obscene?
Ok, obscene they always were, it's too late for forgiveness now
I cannot move, I cannot breathe, I can't evade this anyhow
The aches and pains, all well deserved
My place in Hell has been reserved
Should I confess and break the dam?
Let others judge on who I am?
Should I surrender. know my place?
For failings I did not embrace
Admit my sins, I have no choice
Now, left condemned without a voice
But hopefully, new freedoms wait, where there's a chance I might escape
When brighter fortunes lie in store, a better life may still take shape
Until, at last, I realise that I have got no place to run
It's time to face my punishment for everything that I have done.

Forbidden Fruit

I look at you but cannot touch
I sense your warmth but cannot feel
The things I want, I want too much
The things I need, not mine to steal
Forbidden fruit hangs everywhere
None destined though to comfort me
At times life seems too hard to bear
Forbidden fruit is all I see
Unnoticed as I wander by
Forever I shall walk alone
The fight too hard, I cannot lie
The joys you feel, to me unknown
Forbidden fruit surrounding me
Reminds me what I cannot be.

Last Night I Dreamt Of Somebody Who Doesn't Exist

Last night I dreamt of somebody who doesn't exist
A woman I had never met but I could not resist
But when I woke no sign remained, of the love I'd
always craved
I'd spent the night in Heaven, but my dreams could
not be saved

She held me tight and promised me
She'd never leave my side
I wanted her, she wanted me
My smile grew ever wide
Her windswept hair blew in my face
I revelled in the breeze
She kissed me softly on the lips
I felt so safe, at ease
I marvelled in her presence
Whilst others did the same
But all her focus fell on me
I never learnt her name
Her smile, it lit up all around
Like the sunrise lights the sky
To see perfection in my mind
If only I'd known why

For perfection leads to imperfection
Where disappointment wins the day
Where rejection leads to more rejection
So, I chose to dream and hide away
Instead, I chase the unobtainable
As I choose to put my life on hold
My dreams, my playground, in my head
Left me alone, forever cold

Last night I dreamt of somebody who doesn't exist
Naively, I believed in her and what a life I've missed.

I Might Have Kissed You On The Lips

I might have kissed you on the lips
If only I had not been scared
To face rejection, to take a risk
If only I had been prepared

I might have kissed you on the lips
But deep down, I expected, "No"
Instead, I held you by the hand
And now, I think, I'll never know

I might have kissed you on the lips
But fearful you might lead me on
I backed away and froze in fear
And now, the chance, forever gone

I might have kissed you on the lips
Instead, I looked you in the eye
And dreamt that soon, I'd kiss you, then
I walked away and waved goodbye.

Ghost

Every night he sees her ghost
Then, when he wakes, all hope is gone
The one he felt he loved the most
Was she imagined all along?

Her soothing smile glowed deep inside
That smile was always on his mind
But now, it seems, the dream has died
A love that he will never find

Was she ever even there?
Did she ever hear his plea?
Did she ever really care?
With her, he knows, he cannot be.

Wandering

I'm just wandering
No idea where I'm heading
No plans for where I'm going
No longer am I growing
My focus all defeating
In life, always retreating
Wandering to where?
Perhaps go anywhere
To any place I dare
Perhaps go everywhere
Or maybe go nowhere at all
To a place where I will fall
To a place I'm bound to fail
At last, to end this sorry tale
To keep on going till I rest
To still believe I did my best
Then to collapse into the ground
To be lost and never found
To spend my days and weeks a-pondering
To waste this life of mine just wandering.

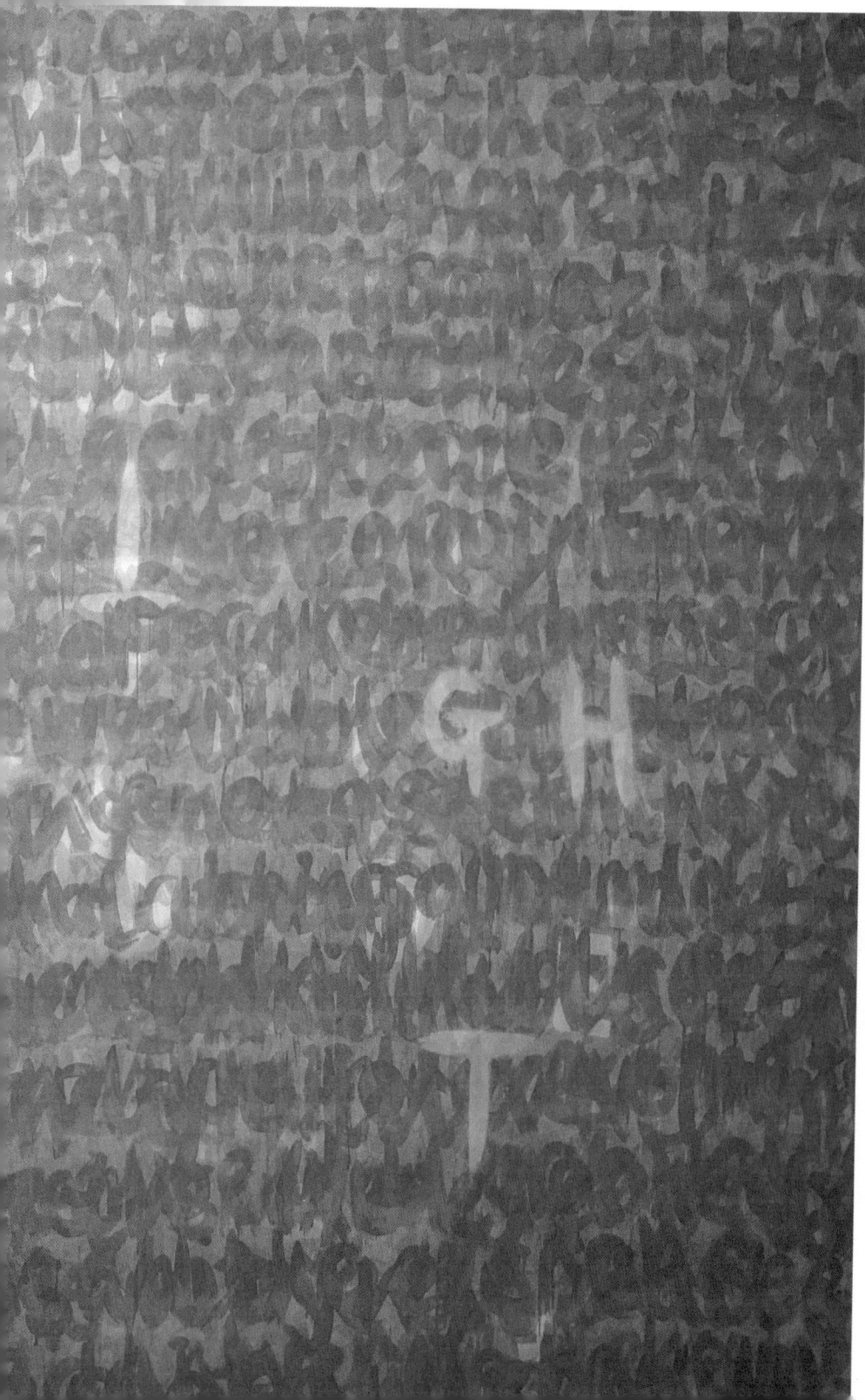

Part Four

The Fading Light

*"The poet lights the light and fades away.
But the light goes on and on".*

Emily Dickinson.

The Fading Light

The fading light cannot be ignored
Nor the wilting flowers or the falling leaves
Or the distant places I have not explored
Where hope once flourished, now nothing breathes
The sun is setting, I too descend
My days succumb to this long goodbye
When the sky falls in, life can never mend
We have grown apart, I do not know why
This my pain to bear and my pain alone
The loss one sided, as I start to slow
All around is laughter, but I've never known
A way to be happy, of life's sweet glow
I have never marvelled at the joys of spring
Or that warm, snug feeling, where contentment stirs
Or the happy memories and the smiles they bring
In the fading light, all nostalgia blurs
These my final steps, on my final task
As I wave goodbye to all I adored
Give me one last chance, this is all I ask
But the fading light, cannot be ignored.

Dull, Dreary Day

Another dull and dreary day
One thousand more are on the way
Too dark outside, inside I hide
The world not mine to plagiarise
The day not mine to terrorise

This mild but dull and dreary day
Where dampness fills the morning air
Her secrets are not mine to share
The day not going anywhere

The light too short, the night too long
For now, at least, I'm feeling strong
But soon, I know, I'll grow so weak
And I will be afraid to speak
I'll blend into her misty air
Dull, dreary day, life isn't fair

I'll contemplate, then sit and wait
For spring to come, for life anew
And only then, I'll be with you
To live the life, I never knew
From far away I'll view it all
Then when I'm destined for a fall
I'll face the world in bold defiance
My world defined by blissful silence.

The Day Before Nothing

Today is the day before nothing
Where lonely nothings await
Today is a day of regret and remorse
Of violent storm clouds which line the horizon
Which leave us dismayed and resigned to our fate

Today is the day of a darkness
A day of crushed hopes and lost dreams
Today is a day which has nothing to say
Of wanton destruction which holds us all back
Of torturous hope framed by vacuous themes

Today is a day without meaning
We dream of escape from this place
We wait for a joy which will never become
We plan for a future tomorrow won't bring
For a disappointment we are destined to face

To a wonder long gone which we'll never replace.

Waiting For Tomorrow

Another sunset on the way
The end of yet another day
I count the hours and days away
Waiting for tomorrow

Another day, devoid of light
Surrendered to my sorry plight
I disappear into the night
Waiting for tomorrow

Another friendship bites the dust
My inner thoughts are not discussed
Consumed by envy and mistrust
Waiting for tomorrow

Another month soon disappears
Whilst watching more successful peers
This carries on for years and years
Waiting for tomorrow

Another decade lost to time
Until I'm way beyond my prime
Too soon, the final bell will chime
Still waiting for tomorrow

Then, when my ending lies in wait
And I've surrendered to my fate
And finally, it's far too late
There will not be a tomorrow.

I'm Tired

I'm tired of the winter
Of this long and lonely night
Of the unforgiving wintry cold
Of nature's icy bite
I'm tired of cloud filled skies
Of fatigue and constant gloom
And I'm tired of dreams abandoned
To this cruel, impending doom

I'm tired, now, of waiting
For the springtime to begin
And I miss the evening sunsets
When I feel a glow within
I'm tired of fleeting sunshine
Of winters spiteful tease
Of the dark and dreary mornings
Of the naked, leaf-free trees

Please hurry, leave me winter
So, my spirit can revive
Let the cherry blossom fill the trees
Let the tulips come alive
No more waiting for renewal
As the winter falls apart
Then I'll feel the darkness leave my soul
As the sunshine warms my heart.

New Dawns

Is this the Spring I've waited for?
A brand-new dawn where dreams come true
A wistful landscape where skylarks soar
A clear horizon where hopes renew
Where swallows dart and fill the skies
I'll watch their dance on sultry days
A spring which leads to summer's prize
Of warmth and wonder and joyful praise

The bluebell woods are ours to savour
With shades of blue, of purple, green
We need to take the time to savour
The cheer in all that we have seen
And when we take the chance to ponder
To bathe in all that warms our heart
To let our minds submerge and wander
Before these final hopes depart

For happiness, we know, won't last
So, take the time to cleanse and mend
The seasons move and change so fast
As new dawns pass and good times end.

Mendip Memories

The evening mist descending
The sun is growing weak
We know that we will not again
Traverse atop Crook Peak
To not again immerse ourselves in the views atop the hill
Remembering those long-lost days when time stood ever still

The long walk, now, is almost done
A ramble away from the end of the day
Where once we'd wander for hours, carefree
Those days now seem a lifetime away
To reach the top of Beacon Batch
The cruel ascent from Rodney Stoke
The track that climbs through Ebbor Gorge
The memories these all evoke

Those peaks now just a distant view
But still so vivid in my mind
Unreachable and out of touch
The treasured memories left behind

Through Stockhill Woods and Priddy Mines
Down muddy paths, 'neath mighty pines
Where ancient folk interred their dead
Where Romans came in search of lead
From Cheddar to Wookey. a place of retreat
A secretive world beneath our feet
The limestone hills we once adored
Where caves and caverns lie unexplored

The rock of ages, forever remained

In Burrington Combe where those words were ingrained
Our presence is fleeting, regrets abound
We grow older and older till we lie in the ground

Then out to sea where we walked Brean Down
Towards the solace of the Mendips end
Across to Steep Holm, which we'll never reach
Our strolls confined to the flats of the beach
Constrained, low lying by life's cruel tune
The triumph of youth gone far too soon

Enriched, I sit by the springs in Wells
Where waters escape the hills above
Awaiting a call, at last, the bells toll
The final chimes of an infinite love
The sadness, aloneness, the feelings of pain
Of all the things we won't do again
I pause and reflect on a wasted past
Of days, I believed forever would last

A future I will be denied
No way to usher back the tide
No right of return, the privilege spent
The joys of the Mendips were only lent

Those places we will not again see
Accept what was will not again be.

The Yew

Slips of yew silvered in the moons eclipse
Conceived to deceive, designed to destroy
In haste, we absorb the juices she drips
A poisonous brew, which assassins deploy

Today, that same tree looks over us still
A path to the heavens, a beacon of light
On the darkest of days as prophecies fulfil
Her sparkle eternal, she shines through the night

Her roots seep deep into dream like states
Where fear of death is forever ingrained
A world of mayhem where evil dictates
Where the yew is the only lifeform sustained

Bringing omens of doom from beneath the soil
Her roots venture further than any man dare
Above on the surface where working men toil
Grim vibes of morality smother the air

It's said Pontius Pilate was born under a yew
In the Fortingall's shade, where he grew, where he
played
Through the innocent childhood, which all of us knew
Till temptations in manhood where he wandered and
strayed

Was the evil harboured in the roots of that tree?
Now surrounded by graves of people long gone
Mortality lurking in you and in me
From dust unto dust as the days linger on

The fear of an ending, forever unknown
A falsehood that we have always been taught
Throughout our struggles, through all that we own
Remembering failures that we never fought

Then, when there's no longer a light from the sky
All we have known will crumble to dust
Even the planets above us will die
Even the stars will one day combust

A sacrificial lamb as we fall to the ground
A superficial ending as our final path is found
Bow down and take our punishment, we face our
judgment day
In waning light, as darkness falls, we join the roots and
fade away.

THE WORLD
THOUSAND MILES
I WILL NEVER

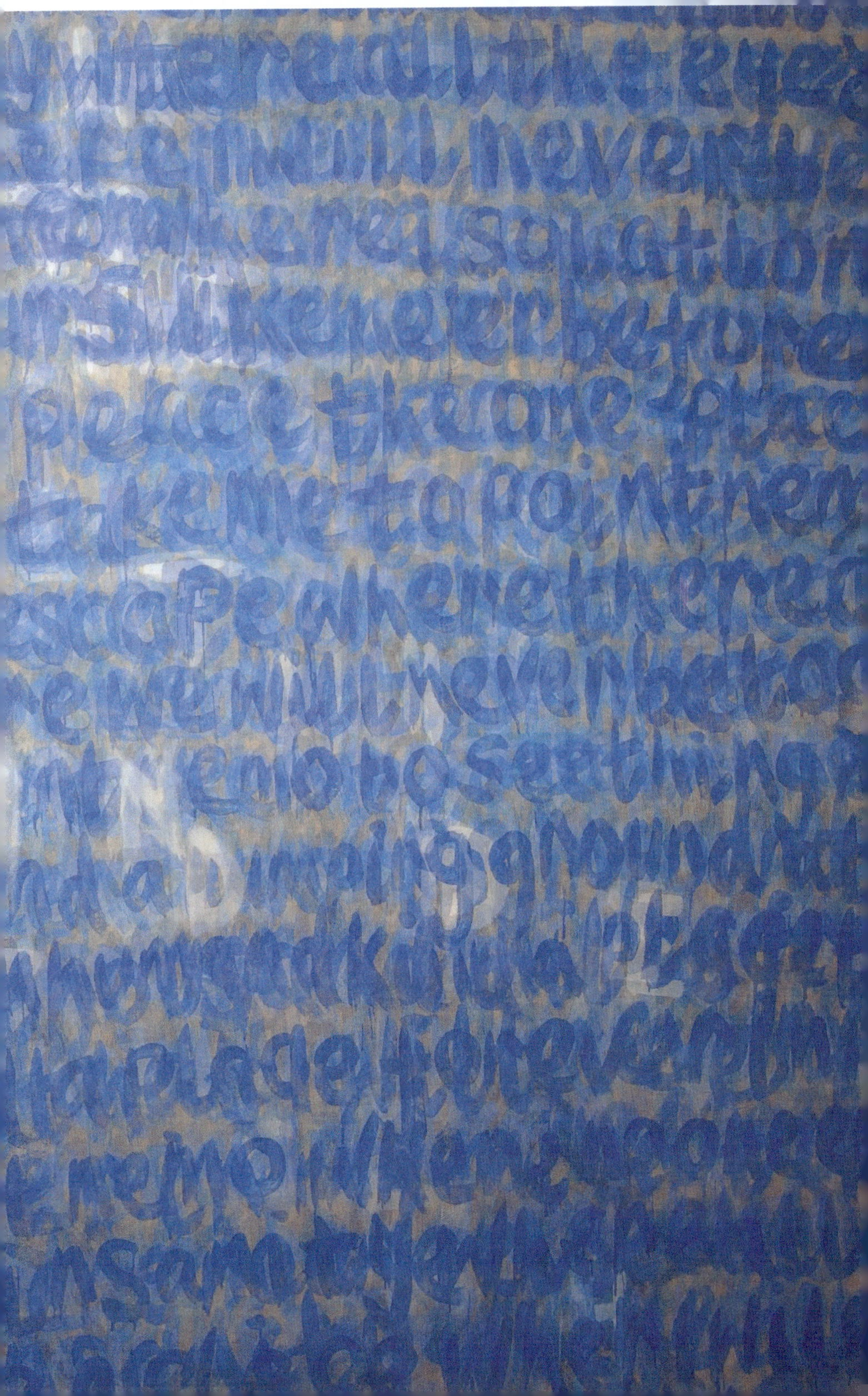

Part Five

The Wild, Wild Wind

"You find out the strength of a wind by trying to walk against it, not by lying down".

C.S. Lewis.

The Wild. Wild Wind

There's a sense of foreboding in the misty morning air
Where the wild, wild wind is calling, as her call grows
ever wilder
 I choose to leave the safety of the cover of the trees
I am in her hands, now harnessed, by the power of
her breeze

I fall on to my knees as the wild wind brings me down
Then, the world and her subjects forced to give in to
their fate
As the war, the grief, the famine and disease begin to
spread
We are all forced to surrender to the whims of the
dead

Her victims, they are chosen- at random, so it seems
Our destiny decided by the wild, wild wind, which
blows
Where nobody is sacred, all are treated just the same
All are victims of her majesty when she's calling out
our name

Where will I be blown?
To a place I've never known
Where will I be blown?
To a place we're never shown
Our paths have crossed, all-purpose lost, no strength
to carry on
The paradise we dreamt of in our lives is now long
gone

But the wild, wild wind, in spite of this, will carry me
on home

Neither friend nor foe, she has no say in how my story ends
So, now, where will I go?
Well, that, I do not know
But regardless, I am certain, I'll be guided by the breeze
Then, the wild, wild wind will bring me back to the shade of mighty trees
To a world I can't imagine, where love is all I see
Where mystery is history; and each one of us is free.

Beyond The Water

Beyond the water
Where life emerges
Rises the power of a mighty God
The tower above me
Centuries of history
I sit here, creating
Where once, they trod

Their shadows fill the holy water
The images and dreams they shared
A paradise is born of beauty
An oasis filled by long lost prayers
Their stories unknown
Their lives too short
Their memories cannot be bought

The power and the majesty
A view of strength to scare us all
A glory to remind ourselves
That they were nothing
Their lives meant nothing
The simple lives of sinful man
Forgotten in God's greater plan

Let me wander in her glory
To walk where long-gone peasants toiled
I praise the splendour that basks before me
Their stories are not mine to tell

Where I view the spring that sits before me
Where I view the waters which forever awe me
Where I view the tower
Where I feel her power

Where I sit in wonder
Where I view the well.

The Weeping Willow

Come weep with me, oh weeping willow
To mourn on days when life moves slow
Cry out when all around is darkness
To weep at worlds, we'll never know

Oh. weeping willow, come surround me
And let your branches wrap 'round me
Your warm embrace, the one we cherish
Engulf me will you, willow tree

But nature chose your role in life
To fall to earth whilst others thrive
They reach up high towards the stars
Whilst you bow down to stay alive

Within this life, all have their purpose
Your role to reach towards the soil
To keep us calm and keep us grounded
Throughout the storm, throughout life's toil.

Waiting For The Snowdrops

I sit and imagine a carpet of white
A view that brings hope of an end to the night
A place where the world is returning to life
Today, I am waiting for the snowdrops

No day more perfect than today
The air crisp cold, a cloudless sky
A view which brings a mortal shine
A dream where snowdrops will soon be mine

Remember life will start anew
The world will soon emblaze in colour
The sun sets later, day by day
Slowly, but surely, spring on the way

Although the icy winds still blow
A hopeful future beginning to grow
A fleeting moment of joy in our fight
Our brief flirtation with a carpet of white.

Cherry Blossom

Where does the cherry blossom go?
When spring is gone
When summer comes
Becomes the fruit, the trees cerise
In autumn too, the fruits are gone
Where do they go? Life moves so slow
But change comes fast
In life we know
That soon we'll pass and what once grew
Will turn to dust, then start anew
So, life continues on this path
Ours just a flicker in the sun
All that's born will leave us soon
All we have will be undone
We'll never understand just why
Or what we are or where we've been
When make believe becomes our truth
Eternity our wildest dream
The truth untrue
Forgotten now
Like we were never, ever, here
And like the cherry blossom blooms
We too will fade. then disappear.

Acker's Grave

The words on his gravestone
Tell of life as a boy
Of a life well lived
Full of wonder and joy
On those long summer days
Which he spent here at play
Where the magic of childhood
Swept all worry away
On the rope swings he'd swing
In the waters he'd dive
In the river at Publow
Never felt so alive
When all seemed much simpler
When life wasn't a chore
When each day was a gift
Now those days are no more
But the wagtails and kingfishers
Still soar in my view
The scene here eternal
In this place which he knew
Too much in life changes
But much stays the same
Forever the gravestone
Will bear Acker's name
Soon we'll be left behind
And time will move on
And one day, like Acker
We too will be gone
But his music continues
And his passions still glow
And so long as the world turns
Then the river will flow.

The Clair De Lune

I lay on my back, looking up to the sky
I watched in amazement as the clouds sauntered by
The world all around, unremembered today
All I saw was the sky and her dazzling display
But I knew that this wonder would soon be cut short
As the call of the reaper, too soon, would hold court
But there, in the moment, I immersed and believed
My mortality beaten, and my soul was reprieved
Then as the sun set and as nightfall set in
And the darkness swept over, I felt fearful within
Until the wind blew, and the clouds disappeared
Up above me the stars, in their glory, appeared
I looked back to a time way before I was born
In my moment of peace there was no time to mourn
Hypnotised by the music of the nights Clair de lune
As the skies came alive in the glow of the moon.

Forever

I return to the spot which once inspired me
The place where Forever Gone was born
Two years have passed and much has changed
Life getting better but still, I'm torn
Surrounded now by overgrown graves
Neglected by the passage of time
My words remembered; their lives forgotten
And me, I'm well beyond my prime
But then I found you, found new meaning
I felt reborn and full of verve
Again, a young man, one last time
To find a love we both deserve

Will you be different than those before?
Will our pasts destroy us before we find more?
When we are gone will we lie together?
Or will we be laid to rest apart
Will we remain together forever?
Ingrained within the other's heart
And if we do not rest together
Will what we have soon fade away?
And where you lie, so soon forgotten
I'll be forgotten far away

But, maybe, then the wind might turn
And blow our ashes back together
And when we're back, beside the other
Then we will rest, as one forever.

THE

TIDES

Then I looked down or around, I would never get to
see.
As I begged for mercy from my God in the hope He
might own me.

Part Six

The Tide

"The lowest ebb is the turn of the tide."

Henry Wadsworth Longfellow.

The Tide

The tide, we know, forever turning
We face the force which drives us on
We reminisce when she reminds us
Of all the times when life went wrong
To sit and watch is life's great pleasure
To let the hours pass us by
To not be bound by rules or judgement
Accept life's faults and don't ask why
The tide, we know, is always changing
Throughout the ups and downs of life
The highs and lows which keep us going
Renew and keep us safe from strife
For all that turns will turn to dust
Or, if we're lucky, maybe gold
The waves are strong and unforgiving
They break our spirit, leave us cold
At other times it's calm and peaceful
The stress and worries fade away
Then back we go to where we started
A past which haunts us every day
Don't fight the rips, don't fight the current
Don't doubt your strength, go with the flow
The tide your friend, the tide your saviour
Embrace her force, then let her go.

White Spring

Immersed in the might of the waterfall
In healing waters which thrill and enthral
Is this the night where day begins?
A paradise where virtue wins?
My mind untroubled by worlds remote
I cleanse, repent to stay afloat
A route I thought I'd never take
A creed I felt I'd never break
But then I broke it
And then endeared it
I idolised it
I never feared it

In meditation, with you, alone
In isolation, my cover blown
Senses are seared
Senses alive
My mind is cleared
As new dawns arrive
Then all ill-feeling, at last, is purged
When all ill thoughts have been submerged
Released from all that's gone before
Then freed from my past in the shade of the Tor.

To Woollard

The bridge is now a ruin
The mill, itself, long gone
But the millpond never left us
And the Chew, it lingers on
Beneath the bridge she rushes
Cavorts across the weir
The sounds abound so heavenly
The source of so much cheer
We enter in the shallows
Wade deeper with each stride
Submerged within the water
We are ready for the ride
To the weir we cling heroically
Till we're ready to let go
Then we're in the swoosh, so fearless
As we join the rivers flow
Safely swept back to the shallows
Where all of this began
Ever since that fateful meeting
We are mermaid and merman
With my eyes closed I imagine
Life will always be this way
When my mind's allowed to wander
Here in Woollard I will stay.

The Lighthouse

Her presence never fades
She'll never leave my side
She shines a bright light through the mist
Through long and cold and lonely nights
No place to hide but still she stays
She guides me through my darkest days

The storms are sent to test us
The current keeps us far apart
But when I am in danger
I see her through her steely glare
No need to worry or beware
I know that she'll forever care
I know that she is always there
Forever by my side

Her inner strength provides my power
My guiding light, each waking hour
Then when the sun begins to set
She'll be the source of all my hope
She'll be the force which helps me cope
She'll save me when my mood is bleak
She'll give me strength when I am weak
Then, when I'm stricken with despair
Her gleaming presence fills the air
She shines a bright light everywhere
I know that she is always there
Forever by my side

Nanjizal

Is this the way to Heaven?
Across the rocks and through the cave
A portal to another world?
To all I want and all I crave?

The tranquil, peaceful mermaid pools
A contrast to the windswept beach
The ruthless ocean keeps me from
A paradise I'll never reach

We cross the rocks to face the swell
To find a place where all is well
Towards a world we'll never know
We will not learn, we'll never grow

When high tide comes, all disappears
The dream is dead, the magic clears
A calmness we're afraid to chase
A truth we cannot know or face
Beyond the cave a land unknown
A world I'd best leave well alone.

Towan

I swam down from Portscatho
Was o'er a mile across the bay
Pre-swim, I'd heard from idle talk
Of dangers on that summer day
"Ice cold winds blow 'cross her sands
Her waters harsh and ever cold"
But on arrival, I would sense
Her welcome not what I'd been told

I'd ventured here some years before
Her windswept sands seemed much the same
But time won't wait for any man
This life is cruel, a heartless game
Near twenty years since I was here
In life, time moves on ever fast
In twenty more I'll be long gone
This trip to Towan could be my last.

Porth Nanven

The path winds down through gorse and ruins
Colours enliven, entice and excite
Sounds of water, rushing, escaping
Race to the ocean with crushing might
Views of yellow flowers awaken
With spring now close, new hope is teased
Up above the cliffs stand steadfast
The valley sheltered; our worries eased

Towards Porth Nanven, dreams come true
Low tide is now; she's in her prime
Soft golden sands meet lapping waves
She's calm for now, evading time
'Cross dinosaur eggs formed aeons past
The stream, she sprints across the beach
I face the rocks, my path much slower
Each step with care until I reach

The cleansing scene where words are written
I stand unfazed, stare out to sea
My thoughts consumed by worlds forgotten
A place of peace where I can't be
For all the beauty now surrounding
Relief too brief, I cannot stay
Back cross the rocks to where I started
Where tears and sadness rule my day.

Remembering Rebecca

Last night I dreamt I went to Manderley again
The scent of salt sea air where I'd loved and lost
before
Remembering Rebecca as the tide began to turn
The still warm sun was setting as the waves lapped
on the shore

In Charlestown I sit pondering - beside the harbour
wall
The Gribbin swiftly fading in a cloud of thick sea mist
Beyond lie long lost secrets of a Manderley now gone
My love for her still lingers, though my heart fights to
resist

Across the bay, not far away, lie fields of ripened corn
Ready to be harvested- with autumn on the way
Samphire, wilting, clings to cliffs from Gribbin to
Polkerris
Sheltering my Manderley from winds that cross the
bay

The crabs marooned in rockpools which sparkle in
the sand
Lie waiting in captivity, held hostage to the seas
command
The tide will turn, come evening all the crabs will be
set free
But nobody can tell me when the tide will turn for me
And if it does, where will it lead? To the place my
heart desires?
Beyond the cliffs of Gribbin, to a land adorned in
fires?

I don't want my days to end in the razzmatazz of
Charlestown
Where tins of sickly fudge hide behind postcard
covers
Where hungry, sunburnt tourists feast on melting ice
cream
All haunted by the stories of abandoned, vanquished,
lovers

I will return to Manderley, I'll swim across the bay
Through fleets of fishing boats, with the dolphins and
the seals
Towards Rebecca's boathouse where I felt an inner
peace
Under cover of the night sky in a dream where
darkness heals
Devoured by a past which was never one I sought
Imagining a Manderley, contentment never found
Then just like Mrs Danvers, I will lose all self-control
I will burn every morsel of nostalgia to the ground
Into the waves, I'll disappear, at last I'll be set free
As the ashes blow towards us, with the salt wind
from the sea.

The Sound Of Water

The music of our lives
A place where we relax and dream
Brings peace and calm
And cleanses minds
Be mighty ocean
Or tiny stream

The babbling brook
The bubbling spring
She talks to me
I hear her sing
The water here
Is crystal clear
Blue, green oasis
Keep me near

I close my eyes
She rushes by
She listens
She glistens
In the glare of the sun
Then as she meanders
She creeps and she crawls
Towards cascades
To glorious falls

Wild and rampant
Is what she becomes
Waterfalls echo
In the gorge below
Then peace restored
Towards the bay
The scene serene

She starts to slow

Swishing and swirling
Pulsates with romance
Ebbs and flows
In her victory dance
The waves are waiting
She reaches the shore
To merge with the sea
A river no more

The reckless ocean
It rages hard
The storms are crashing
With breaking waves
Tempestuous, turbulent
She brings blood and gore
Sometimes her song
Is the song of war

But soon, she'll rest
She'll whisper to me
She'll share her secrets
She'll heal my soul
Tranquil, transparent
My world laid bare
Beside the water
Where I am whole
She rescues me
From depths of despair
Renews my spirit
When troubles are rife
Revived in glory
My mind repaired

The sound of water
Which saved my life.

IN
TO
THE

Part Seven

Into The Light

"We can easily forgive a child who is afraid of the dark; the real tragedy of life is when men are afraid of the light."

Plato.

Into The Light

I don't want to watch you suffer
But I'll never leave your side
If you let me be there just this once
Then I promise I won't hide
I'll support you through your winter
Through the dark and lonely days
When you find it hard to find your way
When you're lost within life's maze
Through your struggles and your troubles
I will lend a helping hand
And when things are bleak as bleak can be
I will pull you out from sinking sand
Then, at last, you'll find your summer
You'll be flying to the moon
And the sun will be your saviour
All you want, will find you soon
You will be reborn and full of life
To be freed from the harm of night
And my smile as wide as the gulf which divides us
As you leave my side and move into the light.

Will I Still Be Here?

When the fight is over
When the battle is won
When good is triumphant
When the pain has all gone

When the sun is rising
When the storms abate
When the rains stop falling
When there's no more hate

When the past is forgotten
When the tide has turned
When the world's full of laughter
When evil is spurned

When we've learnt our lesson
When we fight no more
When love is victorious
When there's no more war

When we're finally happy
When our sufferings cease
When we've found our salvation
When, at last, we've found peace

Then with everyone smiling
When their struggles are through
We'll forgive and forget
As the world starts anew.

The Café

Eccentric paintings on the wall
Hanging baskets overhead
The quirky backdrop soothes my mind
This morning free of doom and dread
The buzz from last night still within
Last night, I feel, my soul was saved
I want to have it all today
I'll let my worries fade away

The Café here no soulless chain
Her aura mends my aching heart
And soon my food is on the way
A perfect day about to start
I watch the strangers, full of joy
The sound of laughter ever warm
A place to rest, enjoy the day
I'll let my worries fade away

The food meets all my wildest dreams
Such love is shared in every meal
My senses sated, the hunger fades
Right here, I take the time to heal
Perhaps this world is in my head
But if that's true then even so
The joy I feel, I feel today
I'll let my worries fade away

From where I sit, I view the church
The tower stands so tall and proud
She reaches to a cloudless sky
The sadness fades, my mind unbowed
I sit alone, admire the view
In solitude, I'm purged of grief

Relax and watch the world at play
I'll let my worries fade away

Displays of cakes and other bakes
The tastebuds teased; how will I choose?
I want them all but make my pick
In this escape, I've found my muse
Indulge the scene, a world at peace
In new beginnings I find release
Content at last, no tears today
I'll let my worries fade away

The savoured blondie, with my coffee
She has me under her sugary spell
Who knew life could taste this good?
I bathe in the flavour and bask in the smell
At last, right here, I've found my place
A loneliness I can embrace
And now, I'm ready for the day
I'll let my worries fade away.

In The House Of God

In the mist I feel a presence
I reminisce of times long past
Tinged with regret at the pace of a life
Which now is disappearing fast

Do I feel forgiveness in the air?
Of a saner world we all can share
Is there foreboding in my heart?
A temptress tearing me apart?

In the house of God, I pause, reflect
On all the places I have been
Awaken, spiritually, cleanse my mind
Of all dark forces I have seen

Will I believe? Can I perceive?
This life was never meant to be
Is there a purpose in this all?
Burnt deep within my heathen soul?

In the house of God I take time out
To reassess and end all doubt
I seek salvation, I sense release
In the house of God, I find my peace

A chance for redemption in the eyes of God
Where those far greater than me once trod
I pray for sanctuary, then freed from my sins
In the house of God, a new story begins.

Today Is A Sunny Day

Today is a sunny day
Where we brave the icy waters, where new lives will
begin
Where I can sense a sparkle and the tingling of the
skin
Which radiates inside my soul and warms me from
within

Today is a sunny day
These holy, healing waters, they cleanse me of my
fear
The sense of place awakens me, my demons
disappear
New feelings of awareness, at last, my mind is clear

Today is a sunny day
Where brave and crazy swimmers, descend the steps
with style
My worries and my struggles are forgotten for a while
Elation washes over me, I see the water smile

Today is a sunny day
With sisterhood and friendship and magic all around
I swim in such serenity; I cannot hear a sound
In the calmness of the water, a new contentment
found.

The New View

The brambles have now taken over the view
And the view from the bench not the view I once knew
Delusion destroyed all the hopes I once held
It was all an illusion, where my sadness rebelled
In my view of the valley and the river below
To the waters I love, still the waters I know
Once written in folklore, now a magnet for lies
Which even the brambles can no longer disguise

But the sun is now shining where it wasn't before
All the feelings I had, I don't feel anymore
The winter is over, a spring has begun
The pain fades away, all my mourning is done

The sunset the same as it always has been
The sadness departs and the new view serene
The sun always rises, in spite of the pain
I am cleansed by the tears and the warm, summer rain

I have found new belief, and I suffer no loss
Just a sense of elation as I venture to cross
The fields from the bench to the river and trees
I am freed from your chains, and I feel so at ease

And as I reach the river, leave the bench well behind
The view again perfect, I no longer feel blind
My mind is now clear, and the river is too
So, I enter the water and begin life anew.

All Was Good

In that moment all was good
The years of sadness disappeared
In autumn, trees came back to life
In warming sun, the pathway cleared
Leaves of brown returned to green
The blossom filled November trees
The evening sun refused to set
The panic gone, my mind at ease
Swathes of snow were melting fast
As arctic winds began to stall
The dark of winter turned to light
The birds of spring resumed their call
The world, at last, returned to life
My spirit, soothed, in time I'd thrive
My heartsick mind soon full of hope
That, maybe, I could still survive
The pain surrendered where I stood
And in that moment, all was good.

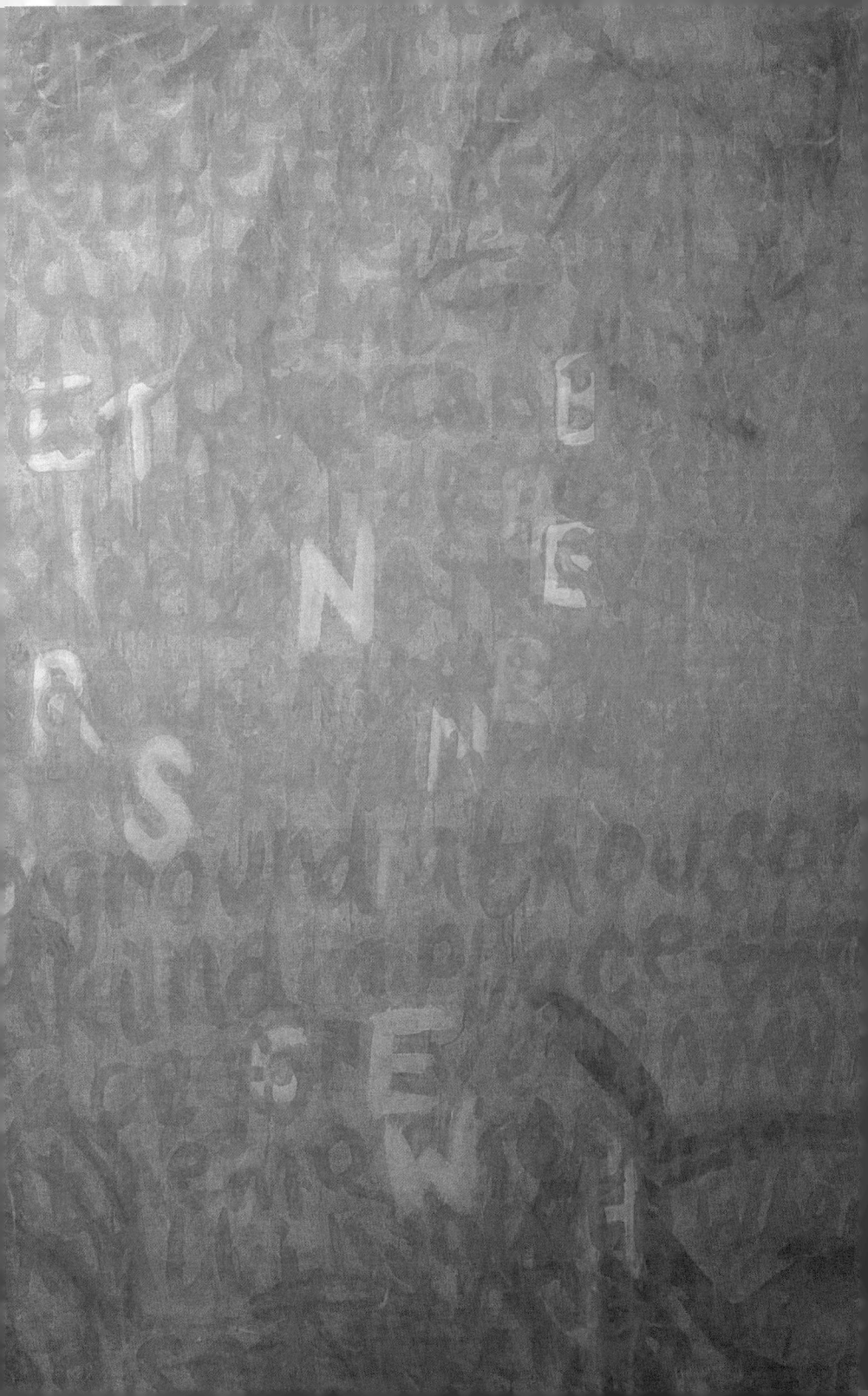

Part Eight

Pastures New

"To-morrow to fresh Woods, and Pastures new."

John Milton.

Pastures New

I'll head to waters, crystal clear
Where land meets sea, where I'm safe from harm
In a place where no one knows my name
Where soft, golden sands mean no need for alarm
Where I'll face and embrace the waves every day
Escaping the demons which stood in my way
Then I'll wave goodbye to the life I once knew
To travel afar, away from you

Today, I believe, is the time to move on
To leave behind everything I have known
To be free of a life which never felt right
To discover a world, I can call my own
With new beginnings surrounding me
I will find a way to set myself free
To start again, to myself be true
To begin a journey to pastures new.

Autumn Blossom

When all within my world is dying
I sense a place of new beginning
A life that I have been reliving
A view I always find forgiving
The trees around me glow with colour
The birdsong, though, seems somewhat duller
Far from the mating calls of spring
Or the joyful choruses summers bring
Instead, I sense impending doom
But still a place where I might bloom

Within my mind is autumn blossom
A darker beauty warms my heart
With winter marching ever closer
I'll tear this bleaker world apart

The autumn blossom none can see
It doesn't grow on any tree
Instead, it flowers in my mind
At times it seemed so hard to find
Then in this world of hope and glory
I start afresh, a brand-new story
I march on now, without a care
As autumn blossom fills the air.

At Last

Where eastern winds blow over me
Exposed to worlds I cannot see
Left vulnerable to a cloud filled sky
A brutal reminder of days gone by

The path long trodden, mistakes forgiven
But not forgotten, they still owned me
In harsh, cold winds I fought to breathe
I faced a world I could not leave

Here, on this spot, I found revival
A road to ruin was all I'd known
But, where I'm sat, I found new ways
I found direction to brighter days

Those brutal winds once held me back
But now the view below has changed
Where in the past I couldn't laugh
I've found a sweeter, happier path

Arise I will, beyond the autumn
My youth is gone, it won't return
But though the days are shorter now
The winter suits me more somehow

The cold it saves me, keeps me grounded
Contentment stirs despite the dark
Where trees stand naked, I bare my soul
At last, in life, I've found my role.

As Beautiful

As beautiful as a happy ending
As the welcome sight of the pearly gates
As beautiful as a Schubert sonata
As a Turner landscape, as the poems of Yeats

As beautiful as a starlit sky
As a velvet moon in a heavenly scene
As beautiful as the morning sunrise
As the evening sunset and all in between

As beautiful as the snowcapped mountains
As the lush green valleys which echo with sound
As beautiful as the winter snowdrops
As the bluebells in spring which carpet the ground

As beautiful as an endless ocean
As the waves which crash on the rocks below
As beautiful as a swim in her waters
As the freedom she brings and the chance to let go

As beautiful as the sound of silence
As the morning mist fills the morning air
As beautiful as the sound of laughter
As the triumph of friendship, as the love we all share

As beautiful as the Garden of Eden
Where soaring eagles complement my view
As beautiful as the world all around us
As beautiful as me, as beautiful as you.

Nirvana

Such a beautiful soul
Such a beautiful smile
Your light shines bright
You are all I see
Today, for the first time
I am free of all doubt
I feel safe from the danger
Knowing there's a way out
You are all I dream of
You are all I desire
A celestial being
From a different sphere
This time, I'm sure
This time I know
My soul is reborn
You are finally here

You take a walk
I follow you
You wait till I am by your side
Your aura spreads so far and wide
The warmth and love which you provide
In this nirvana you will be my guide

I never believed such perfection could be
Right in front of my eyes
Stood waiting for me.

As Yet Unwritten

So little I have said but so much is left to say
The words, as yet unwritten, will they see the light of
day?
When words will not be spoken in the way I'd like them
to
When I struggle to communicate just what I feel for you
If only life were simple, if you never left my side
If every day was perfect and my dreams were not
denied
But, that little bit of magic, it gives me strength and
hope
It keeps me going through the night, gives me what I
need to cope
Then our past will be forgotten, all our sadness will be
through
And the words, as yet unwritten, will be written just for
you.

Riders On The Storm

The doors to the world, wide open again
Where once they were closed in a world full of pain
As we take in the view that fills our surrounds
We've ascended to heaven; our love knows no bounds

Our lives have not been easy
The days have been too hard
Bruised egos, broken minds, all our memories are
scarred
And marred by tragic stories of years spent on the run
Escaping from a world which had never seen the sun
But everything is changing now on top of Knowle Hill
Where the view is one of hope, one where time is
standing still

We view where Stone Age man long ago built Stanton
Drew
Then far below, deep in the valley flows the River Chew
We see the lake and then beyond to where the Mendips
rise
Into sun- kissed, blue and cloudless, everlasting
lovestruck skies

Your spirit taking over me
I feel your electricity
Consuming everything I see
In all the things I hope we'll be
For we are the riders on the storm
We feel no reason to conform
We are the riders on the storm
In this new world we will reform
We are the riders on the storm
Through the longest night I will keep you warm

We are the riders on the storm

And I promise you, a better future
As we wave goodbye to a loveless past
Those days, I promise, will be forgotten
I promise you they will not last

For we are the riders on the storm
I'll stay here by your side forever
We are the riders on the storm
And we will face the waves wherever
We are the riders on the storm.
We will always ride the storm together
We are the riders on the storm
Through the longest night, I will keep you warm

We are the riders on the storm.

Beyond The Altar

To not be drawn by creed or purpose
Instead, to look beyond the shrine
An exit to another cosmos
Beyond the altar, what's really mine?

The glory of a brand-new dawn
Reveals the beauty of a rising sun
Where history defines our present
Where all we've worked for will be undone

Who designed such Majesty?
Who created such perfection?
Our lives may seem implausible
When we've been left without direction

So much has happened in this place
And much of it, so long ago
And whilst it took place on this spot
Was nothing like the world we know

New revelations lose all meaning
No sense of place, there is no "here"
We gain a taste for new perspective
In everything that we hold dear

To re-imagine how we live
To sanctify in praise and glory
Ours not to judge the lives of others
Ours not to tell, tis not our story

To know those times will not return
To not believe the lies we're sold
Beyond our minds and understanding

We're left bereft, forever cold

Beyond the altar, what awaits us?
Beyond this world and all we know
Beyond our own imagination
Beyond where we can ever go.

The Mist Has Now Cleared

The mist has now cleared
New views are explored
I look to the skies
My faith is restored

The boats in the channel
Roll by one by one
The sandbanks exposed
Awaiting the sun

As I start believing
The sun starts to shine
The beauty astounds me
This world is all mine

A silence surrounds me
Now, nothing is feared
The world is at peace
The mist has now cleared.

THE
PO

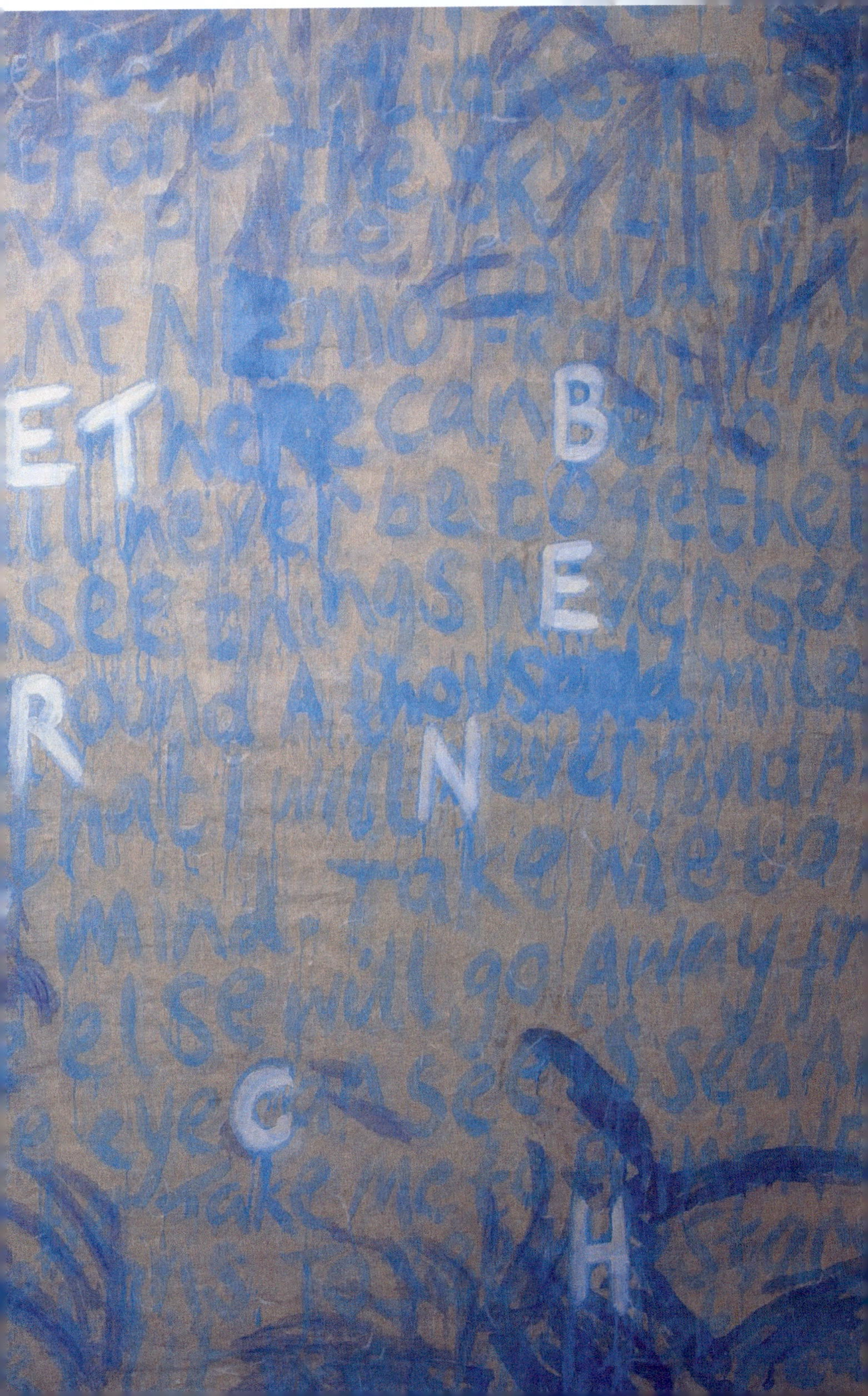
There can Be no
never be together
see things never see
round A thousand
will never find
take me
mind
else will go Away
eye can see

The Poetry Bench

I see the bench which stirs my passion
Where a water flees from high above
Her healing music never-ending
I seek salvation where all is love

All around me, up above me
Watched over by an absolute power
Sounds surround of heavenly birdsong
Which comforts me each waking hour

Who has stood here in the past?
Who has sat where I find peace?
Thoughts reflected on this spot
Who, right here, has sought release?
What did those pilgrims come to seek?
Of what were they allowed to speak?
In search of wisdom, liberation
Worlds fuelled by their imagination

This the seat where I confess
Where I express, where more is less
In the pool, I see reflection
In the calm, I find redemption
Twilit shadows of divinity
Forge a life beyond infinity
Beyond the water, words eternal
Where I sat, composed this journal

Trees of centuries, hidden, solitary
Feed joy head in deep tranquility
Freed from all life's doubts I ponder
My path engraved, yet still I wander

Epilogue

The Poetry Bench

"Life isn't about finding yourself. Life is about creating yourself".

George Bernard Shaw.

The Poetry Bench

I see the bench which stirs my passion
Where water flees from hills above
Her healing music never-ending
I seek salvation where all is love

All around me, up above me
Watched over by an almighty power
Sounds surround of heavenly birdsong
Which comforts me each waking hour

Who has stood here in the past?
Who has sat where I find peace?
Thoughts reflected on this spot
Who, right here, has sought release?
What did those pilgrims come to seek?
Of what were they allowed to speak?
In search of wisdom, liberation
Worlds fuelled by their imagination

This the seat where I confess
Where I express, where more is less
In the pool, I see reflection
In the calm, I find redemption
Twilit shadows of divinity
Forge a life beyond infinity
Beyond the water, words eternal
Where I sat, composed this journal

Trees of centuries, hidden, solitary
Feed my need in deep tranquillity
Freed from all life's doubts I ponder
My path engraved, yet still I wander

In victory I soon forget
My mind is purged of all regret
Then, when I've found my inner peace
Inspired, I write my masterpiece

Into the water, in my dream
I find a place where I redeem
Empowered by all I have got
The magic pulls me to this spot
I find the words, they come to me
Enthralled by everything I see
Enchantment everywhere I look
In every word of every book

And on I go, I reap and sow
These verses speak of all I know
Where all my thoughts are set in stone
In solitude, I'm not alone
The bench where I just sit and write
The star that shines the brightest light
Then, finally, I'm quenched and fed
And all I want to say is said.

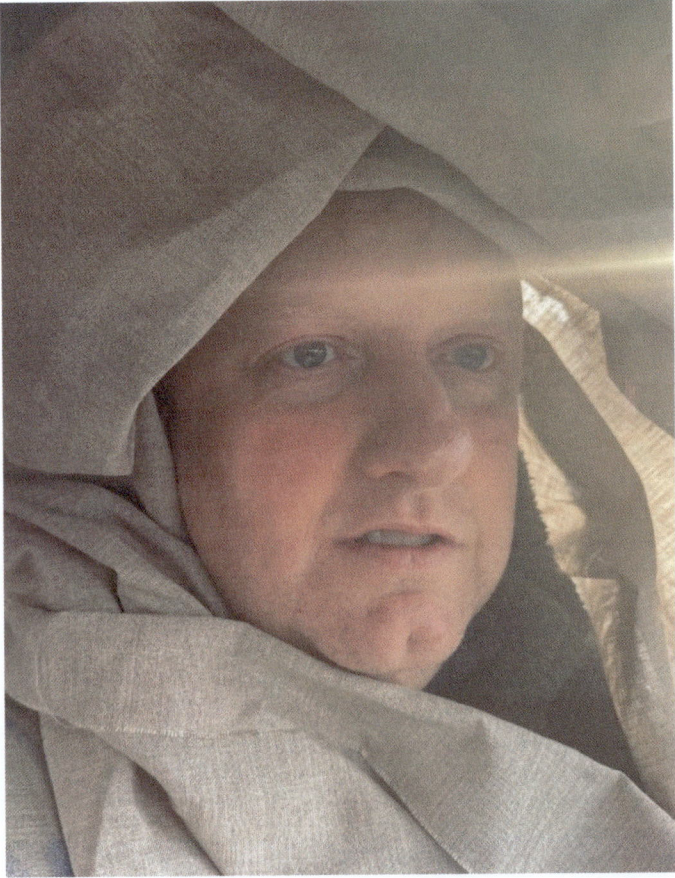

"And all I want to say is said".

Photograph on page 9 courtesy of Sheila Selby

Printed in Dunstable, United Kingdom